THE CALM BENEATH THE STORM

DONAL NEARY SJ

The Calm
beneath the Storm

REFLECTIONS AND PRAYERS
FOR YOUNG PEOPLE

LOYOLA UNIVERSITY PRESS

First published 1983 by
Veritas Publications
Dublin, Ireland

North American edition 1984 by
Loyola University Press
3441 North Ashland Avenue
Chicago, Illinois 60657

Typography by Liam Miller
Cover design by Carol Tornatore
Cover photo by George A. Lane, S.J.

Library of Congress Cataloging
in Publication Data

Neary, Donal.
The calm beneath the storm.

1. College students—Prayer-books
and devotions—English. 2. Catholic
Church—Prayer-books and
devotions—English. I. Title.
BX2373.S8N43
1984   242'.63   84-11220
ISBN 0-8294-0470-8 (pbk.)

CONTENTS

1
PRAYING WITH YOUR SENSES

1 VISION

I like that scene, Lord;
It's one of my favourite places.
I thank you for the colours of the sea, the sky,
    the sand,
And for the peacefulness that such a view brings.
Thanks, Lord, for the gift of sight;
For my eyes, so intricate in their creation,
Carriers of pleasure and joy.

I see so much beauty and life:
    the smiles and faces of friends,
    creativeness of art,
    red of a sunset,
    glow of a dawn,
    photos I cherish,
    films I've enjoyed,
    the sympathy and love I've seen in
        another's eyes,
    the look of love I give in return;
For all this I'm thankful, Lord.

Make me sensitive, too, to all the suffering I see;
Open my heart, as well as my eyes,
    to the wide eyes of starvation in the faces
        of children,
    to the hopeful look of the lonely.

I want to turn away my eyes;
I want to turn away my heart.
Give me the courage to look long and know the
    pain of others;
Give me new sight to see beneath the surface
Of those whose action causes hurt.
May I see them as you see them:
Children of God,
Struggling with many problems.
I pray that I may see, really see.
Thank you, Lord, for my sight.

2 HEARING

That piece of music moved me, Lord.
Thanks for all the sounds I like:
    different music,
    wildlife and country noises,
    echoes of laughter and love,
    the sound of my name being called.
Thanks, Lord, for the gift of hearing and
    listening.

Thanks for the people I have listened to with
    respect;
Thanks, too, for those who have heard me;

Listening, hearing and learning,
Exchanging ideas and feelings,
Fostering sympathy and love.

Help me, Lord, to use this gift in your service:
    to listen with compassion,
    to hear without judging,
    to listen without condemning.
I want to be able to listen between the words,
To hear the joys and struggles of another.
I want to help myself and the other to grow in
    openness.
I want to fully hear her meaning.
Restrain the curiosity in me that invites gossip,
Let me take no pleasure in the weaknesses of
    others,
And may I never fall into the trap of rejoicing in
    someone else's misfortune.
Help me to listen with love and understanding.

Thank you, Lord, for the gift of hearing and of
    listening.

3 SMELL

I hardly notice the sense of smell, Lord.
I thank you for it; it is a gift.
Wildlife smells, flowers and perfume:
For these I thank you, Lord.

Let the fragrance of many moments
Remind me of the fragrance of your love.

Let your love spread through my being
Like the scent of a morning rose.
In enjoying what savours of goodness in your
    creation,
I praise you, Lord.
I am hurried in the world of exams and work;
Don't ever let me become immune to the scent
  of your world.

I pray too, Lord, for those who are deprived of
  this pleasure;
For those whose environment smells of
      violence and death,
      the stench of bombs,
      the garbage of a city's waste,
      the odour of illness,
      the pollution of our skyspace.
Lord, be praised for the sweet beauty of
  everyday things.
Lord, I praise you by letting the fragrance of
  your creation fill my life.

Thank you, Lord, for the sense of smell.

4   TOUCH

I'm thankful, Lord, for the touch of a friend's hand,
      for the hug of sympathy and friendly
          warmth,
      for the embrace of love and care.
I'm thankful for the people whose lives touch
  mine with friendship.

I recall, Lord, the touch of the hands that helped
  me grow from childhood to this day:
The touch of parents and friends that meant
  security and love;
The touch of a friend whose presence cheered me
  when I was sad;
The touch of encouragement when I was afraid;
The touch of sympathy when I was unhappy.
I thank you, Lord, for this gift;
You have touched me many times with
  your own presence
Though the goodness of others.

I remember the touches that wounded me,
That still smart in my memory;
Help me to forgive the lasting sting of hurt,
  insult or rejection.

Help me, Lord, to use this gift in your service,
To nurture your love among us.
Let me not exploit the loneliness and vulnera-
  bility of others;
Let my touch be a touch of care, compassion
  and kindness;
Let it be a touch of joy and freedom;
And in all the touches, embraces and precious
  moments of warmth,
Let me remember that I am meeting one made
  from love,
In the image and likeness of a loving God.

Thank you , Lord, for the gift of touch.

[11]

5 WORDS

Thanks, Lord, for that conversation;
I really feel I got myself across.
I wanted to let her know that her love means a
    lot to me,
And I wanted to tell her something more about
    myself.
Thanks, Lord, for words, for the gift of speech.

With words I have opened my heart to another;
With words I have let another enter into my
    experiences.
At times my words have been lies and gossip.
Thanks, Lord, and sorry.

Help me, Lord, to use the gift of speech in your
    service:
To build up the goodness of others by what I
    say to them;
To brighten their reputations by what I say
    about them;
To speak in care, not cynicism, of others;
To be interesting, not boring;
To speak with a sense of humour and fun;
And, also, to know when to keep my mouth
    shut.

I pray, Lord, for those who cannot speak:
For those who are disabled;
For men and women whose free speech is
    forbidden by hostile regimes;

For those too shy and insecure to speak about
  themselves;
For all who suffer because they have spoken
  out in the cause of justice.

I want to use this gift in your praise, Lord;
To be able to speak of you
And grow in my relationship with you;
To praise you for your goodness in my life;
To spread your message among your people

Thank you, Lord, for the gift of speech.

POSTSCRIPT

The prayers of the preceding chapter introduce you
to praying with your senses — from the things we
see, hear, smell, and touch, and with the power of
words.

Our senses introduce us to the world of other
people and of God. The first way we come to know
anybody is through our senses: we see a person,
hear his voice, touch her hand. Then, if we look
deeply at what's around us, we can see in a view a
sign of God's beauty and care, or see a man or
woman as a child of God. The things we see and
hear can be ways of learning more about God and
our relationship with him.

Often we only half-see or half-hear the things
around us, or we miss the meaning of what we see
and hear. The sound of war can be an occasion to

pray for peace, to hear the cry of Christ in the cry of the wounded, to see his loneliness in the lonely look on the face of a bereaved man or woman. The method of praying like this is to see and hear more fully what God is communicating to us in ordinary moments.

The very activity of seeing, hearing, tasting, touching, or even smelling can be a prayer without words. Just to enjoy the sight of a beautiful sunset can be a prayer in itself. To hear some beautiful music, to smell a fragrant rose, or to hear the cries of God's people can be a prayer. Our senses are "gateways to praying", a means of reaching the presence of God in our hearts.

Make your own prayers along the lines of the prayers of this section. Every moment is filled with sounds and sights which can be signs of God. When we really know that God is active and present always, then everything becomes, to the person of faith, a sign of his presence.

2
PRAYING WITH EXPERIENCES

6 SOMEONE I NOTICED ON THE PATHWAY

He was in the ambulance, the doors not yet
    closed.
As he looked down the street I could see him;
He seemed lonely, downhearted,
An old man about seventy-five,
With a stoop, and a stick in his hand.

Is he alone?
Will family or friends visit him?
Maybe he'll be thinking over his life:
        its sad times,
        ambitions achieved,
        regrets.
Will he feel alone in his illness, as death comes near?

Lord, we often feel alone in the world:
        the child scared in the night when the
            lights are out;

the young person whose love affair has
    broken up;
the husband who thinks his wife has changed;
the woman whose husband has died.
And I know, Lord, that even when we are
  communicating with one another,
We can feel alone,
For we are made with a desire to share life with
  one another.
We also desire, deep in our hearts, to be one
  with you;
Our longing for love and companionship
Is like our longing for union with you.

It's not only in old age, Lord, that I need your
    presence and your company;
It's not only in the ambulance that I need you
  to comfort me;
I need and want your presence every moment
  of my days and nights.
Help me, Lord, to know that you are near,
That you are present with me in my aloneness.
Be near that man too, Lord, in the ambulance;
He needs you, he's alone.

7   BELFAST PRAYER

Lord, these sounds are frightening:
    helicopters buzzing overhead,
    ambulance sirens screaming,
    the noise of a plastic bullet,

the moan of injury,
    the cry of bereavement.
Lord, these are the sounds of our city;
I want to remind you that they are the sounds
    of your city, too.

Help us, Lord,
Heal us,
Make us hunger for peace —
Or is it worth praying for peace at all?

Lord, we are choked with anger at the
    sight of the maimed child,
Mistrust of empty political words,
Fear that loved ones will be hurt,
And the crippling numbness that we live in a
    helpless land.
It's so tough to face what's going on,
So frustrating to work for peace.

These are the deep-down war-worries I bring
    to you, Lord.
Give us, in this troubled city and land,
The peace of heart that even city-peace cannot give;
        reconciliation instead of anger,
        companionship in our fears,
        hope enlivening that awful numbness.

I wonder all the time:
Why are people of goodwill so estranged?
Catholic and Protestant, Roman and Reformers.
Is it not possible to follow the God of love
    without hatred?

Lord, where are you?
Answer us.

The only answer I get, Lord, is the sense of
        your presence,
        healing,
        hungering,
        hoping.
In the prayer groups, political groups, peace
    groups,
I sense your dying and rising among your people:
Dying in the moments of violence and the skin-
    searing shrapnel;
Rising in the resolves for reconciliation and the
    pleadings for peace.

I hear your cry and your call:
        your cry for help,
        and your call to help.
That's all the answer I have;
It will do for another day.

8   UNEMPLOYMENT

I'm out of work, Lord;
I'm looking for a job, and as the weeks go on
I'm beginning to say, "I am unemployed".
Three months now since the last job folded up:
I was hopeful at first, but the longer I'm out,
The harder it seems to get another job.

[18]

"We'll be in touch", or "Work is scarce" — how
    often have I heard that?
The government promises jobs;
My name is with Manpower.

Long hours of boredom, searching, growing
    depression;
One rejection after another.
Why am I treated like a problem because I have
    no job?
I can work, but I feel that no one wants me.

I hate this "no use" feeling, and I loathe the
    sight of the dole queue.
At other times I feel really angry:
Some people have two jobs.
Will this go on for ever, Lord?

Do you care?
About small things like a job?
I'm sure you do.
Help me meantime, Lord, not to feel worthless;
Let me know that your love is still within me;
Let me know that I still have worth as a child
    of God;
And, please, help me to get a job.

9 ANNIVERSARY OF DEATH

Today, Lord, is my dad's anniversary;
Five years now.
It was all so sudden.
I can never forget my disbelief
When I knew I would never see him again;
      never see the smile I liked so much,
      never hear his voice,
      never feel his encouragement,
      never wonder at his silences and his
          worries,
Never again have those rows which seemed
  always so final,
Yet lasted less than a day or two.

I know, Lord, that today I could get very sad,
I could get into a bout of self-pity;
But at least when I remember him I relive the
  good things.
I miss him very much,
But I am thankful that he lives on in my love.

Why did he have to die?
Oh, I know we'll all die, but why just then?
We were young, my mother needed him: Why?
I was angry with you, Lord,
Painfully puzzled why it had to happen to us,
But somehow, sometimes, I feel you are near
  us through it all.

Help me when the loneliness seems too much
  to bear;
I don't feel positive all the time.

Help me not to be bitter or afraid;
Help me to know that your love and strength
　　will sustain me;
That his prayers in his home with you can
　　carry me through.
There's an emptiness in my heart,
A deep void that cannot be filled.
Fill that emptiness, Lord, with hope and
　　confidence.
There's a temptation to fill it with bitterness,
　　　or with guilt that I wasn't kinder to him,
　　　or with intolerance of my family's
　　　　　loneliness.
Fill the emptiness, Lord, with trust
That you are a companion on the journey
　　to a new life;
That he is with you, safe in your love and praying
　　with us;
And let death have no hold over us.
With you we somehow conquer death and break
　　through to life.

I pray, Lord, for my mother:
The loneliness must be more painful for her.
I can see it in her eyes when she thinks I'm not
　　looking,
Or when there's a song playing which they both liked,
Or late at night when the darkness stretches on,
Or when we all go out.
Lord, fill her emptiness too,
In the way that only you can.

I pray that she may find consolation in the love
    they shared
And in your presence now.

And I pray for my brothers and sisters.
We talk about him a lot, but not often of how
    we are in ourselves.
I'd like to help but not intrude.
I pray for them, Lord;
Make my heart open to them,
Especially to be aware when their own
    loneliness and fears
Are making them irritable and difficult.
Help me to understand them,
To be your presence and nearness with them.

10   AFTER SUCCESS

Thanks, Lord, for the success in those exams.
I feel a burden lifted and can breathe freely
    again.
The last few weeks were tense:
Forgive my intolerance of others.
It now seems worth the effort:
    the hours of study,
    the parties I refused,
    the time spent with boring texts,
    the sunshine I missed.
Thanks.

I can see now the point of the hours of patient
    plodding.
It's like seeing the view from a mountain top,
And the climb through the fog was worth it.
I can see now that you were there all the time,
Friendly companion, peace of mind.

May this success be in your service, Lord;
May it lead me into genuine gratitude to you;
May it lead, too, into sincere sympathy and help
For others whose efforts did not give the same
    success.

11 AFTER FAILURE

Lord, I don't even feel like praying now:
I failed the exam.
I am disappointed that I didn't get the results I
    need,
Angry that I didn't work harder,
Jealous, too, of those who passed.

Help me now,
I need your help.
Help me to believe in myself;
Just now my failure makes me feel all bad.

12 SINFULNESS

Lord, I have sinned;
I have been weaker than I thought;
I have failed you.

I feel guilt,
    shame,
    anger;
At what I have done.

Lord, I know that your friendship is a forgiving
    friendship;
    help me to believe this more fully
    help me to forgive myself,
    help me to make up this harm,
    help me to heal this hurt.

I pray that I can really believe in your forgive-
    ness;
This will make me truly thankful to you.

13 QUARREL WITH A PARENT

I feel bad, Lord, about the quarrel with my
    mother.
We both got angry and said things that hurt;
We didn't mean to.
At times the frustration of close intimacy
Dulls the love we have for each other.

She says she wants what is good for me,
But I too need to be heard,
To be trusted as a person in my own right.
I know that just now I feel resentful,
A bit hateful,
But I also thank you for her and everything
    she means to me.
Maybe this bad time will lead to a reconciliation,
And deepen the love between us.

Lord, change my bitterness into understanding.

14   IT'S DIFFICULT TO BELIEVE

It's difficult to believe in you, Lord.
Look at the sufferings of so many innocent
    people;
Look at sickness, poverty and the ravages of
    neglect.
Is this your world, Lord?
Is this your creation?
Are you outside its tragedies and its outrages?
Are you responsible?
They say the world is in your hands;
You seem far away when I call for help.

You say, Lord, that you are loving.
Help me to believe this —
I want to.
May I never become so immersed in doubts
That I fail to grow in faith.

May these doubts lead me
To a new knowledge of your goodness,
To a new understanding of your ways.

Lord, I believe; help my unbelief.

15 WHERE ARE YOU, LORD?

God, I find it difficult to believe in you.
You seem so distant;
I never hear your voice,
I never see your face.
People are suffering from hunger, homelessness
    and violence:
Where are you?
Others seem so certain about you, so sure;
What's wrong with me?
Are you near in the world of money and power?
Where are you in a world that doesn't love or
    care?

Sometimes it's easy to find you in the
    countryside.
In the rock-like strength of the mountain,
Or the peace of the valley,
You touch us with your presence.
But what about bad housing, concrete jungles,
    polluted air?
What about violence, murder, starvation,
    sickness?
Where are you, Lord, in a world

Where babies die each day of malnutrition,
And marriages flounder from houselessness?

I know there are moments when I have found
    your presence.
I think you are present when someone cares
    and helps;
There's a glimmer in the misery.
It's a touch of your love, a sign of your presence.
I expect you to be outside the world,
But you're right in it,
You're in the thick of things.

You're among the starving,
Suffering with them and saving them.
You're among the homeless,
Neglected with them and consoling them.
You're within the broken marriage,
Hurting with them and healing them.

You are suffering, Lord, with those who suffer:
Not just observing it, but suffering;
Not just suffering, but courageously accepted it;
Not just accepting it, but transforming it;
Not just transforming it, but working to lessen it.

Can I believe that the glimmer in the misery is
    your light,
Your risen hope,
Your eternal promise?

Lord, I believe; help my unbelief.

16 CONFUSION

Lord, I'm so mixed up;
There seem to be so many aspects to my
   personality:
With teachers and parents I am one person,
With friends I am another.

I want to do good, to follow you;
But at other times
I'm mean,
I cheat,
I use others for my own advantage.
You see, I'm a rag-bag of things.
Who am I, Lord, anyway?

I want to please my parents,
Yet I want to be myself.
I don't want to hurt my elders,
Yet I want to be independent.
I don't want to seem rebellious,
Yet I want to be alive and spontaneous.
Tell me, Lord, how to find my true self.

Help me, Lord, to grow in confidence,
To conquer insecurity.
I know you understand who I am:
Help me to know myself, forgive myself,
And value myself as you do.

Lord, give me patience
With my growing-up.
Give me confidence

That within these different aspects of my
    personality
I will discover a self that I can accept and love.
As I discover myself, make me an instrument
For the knowledge of your love
And the spread of your Gospel.

17 FEAR

There are times, Lord, when I feel afraid,
Like floundering in the deep end of a
    swimming pool,
Or being lost in the dark,
Or feeling like a stranger on a new estate.
A feeling of tension or darkness;
It's hard to give it a specific cause or even a
    name,
But I know it's in me, and I wonder why.

I feel afraid to trust someone with a secret;
I am nervous that they might let me down.
I feel anxious about that interview,
Because I might make a fool of myself.
I feel afraid to offer friendship to others
In case they reject me.
I'm afraid of many things, many situations:
        fearful of my opinions being laughed at,
        fearful of my friendship being dumped,
        fearful of feeling foolish,
That's me.

Let me pause, Lord, and know what my fears
    mean.
They are not wrong,
But they often prevent me from doing
    something worthwhile:
        showing some kindness,
        breaking out of a rut,
        or saying what's right in my group.
Fears are like a red light at a junction, warning
    me of something,
But if the lights never go green, the traffic gets
    stuck;
And if my fears control me, I never live freely.

Let me be aware of my fears, Lord, for what
    they are worth.
Help me to overcome them so they don't
    shatter my confidence.
At times I feel so empty,
Like a well with no end,
Or a withered leaf;
But help me to know you love me, fears and all.

18 JEALOUSY

When I heard that about her today, Lord, I
    really felt jealous.
I always wanted to be her friend, and now I've
    lost her.
The feeling eats me up —
I can appreciate the phrase "green with
    jealousy".

I feel angry,
Full of resentment,
And blame myself for not working harder
To get what I wanted.

It makes me want to take it out on her new
    friend,
To show him that I'm as good as he is.
Or else I get into a mood of self-pity
And think my world has collapsed around me.
Lord, help me with this jealousy:
I wanted to feel less resentful than I do.

I know I'm struck by jealousy because I feel
    inferior to others.
I feel I'm not special enough to attract someone's
    friendship,
Not successful enough to be wanted.
It's a question of accepting myself,
Accepting, too, that I can't own anyone.
Another's friendship is their gift to me, not my
    right.

Help me, Lord, to know my own value,
And to know that rejection by one person
Doesn't mean that I'm worthless.
Help me to appreciate what I've got,
Rather than lament what I haven't got.
Help me, Lord, to rejoice in the good fortune of
    others,
And to love them as you do.

19 SELF-CONFIDENCE

Lord, I really need your help:
I feel so lonely, so isolated;
I want to make friends, but I can't.
I know I have some friends,
But I sometimes feel that they don't like me,
Or that if they got to know me well, they would
    stop liking me.
I'm like a wave thrown up on the seashore
That can't get back into the flow.

My best friend seems to like my company, after all;
We make a difference to each other's lives.
Thanks for that.
Thanks, too, for my sense of humour.

Help me, Lord, in times of doubting my worth.
Remind me of my good qualities,
Let me see in myself what others admire in me,
Let me give you thanks for what's good in me,
Rather than moping about what might be.

Thanks, Lord, for me.
Thanks for shaping,
Moulding,
Bringing to birth
What's good in me.
Nurture me and build me up.

Help me to encourage others in their goodness.

Let me rejoice in the belief that we are made in
  your image.
Give us confidence in our own goodness,
So that we can grow in our friendships.

20 GOD, WHO ARE YOU?

God, who are you?
It all seemed so simple in childhood:
God, a gentle Father, and Christ, the friendly
  Saviour.
But now it's all questions.
The experiences of my life make me ask questions.
I don't see you, and I wonder where you are;
I see horror heaped upon horror,
And I wonder why your love is not at work in
  our world.
My own life is so full of struggles and doubts
That I despair at times;
And there's so much suffering among the
  people I know
That I wonder at the meaning of human life.
I admit, Lord, that my own faith in your
  goodness is shaken
By hurts in my own life:
Death, broken friendships, illness,
Make me question who you are;
Fears and anxieties about my future, about
  failures and weaknesses,
Make me question who I am.
Will I ever be able to love?
Will I be a victim of the evil in our society?

Will the lure of money, sex, and power bewitch me?
Will I fail?
Will you fail me?

God, where are you?

You are a mystery;
Everyone I know is a mystery.
If a person is so hard to understand,
It only stands to reason that you, our God, are
   even more so.
I can't know another person completely;
I can't know you completely.
Let my relationship with you be a mystery to
   be lived out,
Rather than a puzzle to be worked out;
A hand to be held,
Rather than a mind to be fathomed;
An adventure to be undertaken,
Rather than a problem to be solved.

21 FORGIVING SELF

It's hard to forgive myself, Lord.
I often think of the ways I've let you down or
   harmed others.
I feel so ashamed when some of these
   memories come to mind,
I wish I could draw the curtains on myself and
   not be seen.

The harsh words, not always true, spoken
    about others;
The disloyal remarks about a good friend who
    has just hurt me;
The encouragement to someone to drink too much;
The drugs I passed around;
The money stolen or cheated;
I just ask why I do these things —
I know they are wrong.
I could have done good, but I didn't.

The memory is like heavy baggage I carry with me,
A blot on the pages of my life-story —
A blot that stares me in the face and depresses me.
It's a bitter grudge I bear against myself.

Lord, do you forgive?
Do they forgive?
I don't know,
But I know that behind the curtain I draw on
    myself,
I need some sort of cleansing.
It's hard to forgive myself,
Because I must admit that I was wrong.
No space now for excuses: I confess my
    wrongdoing.
I ask you to pierce through this curtain of
    shame with your forgiveness,
To carry my baggage,
To erase the blot,
Then I can begin to forgive myself.

Replace my denial of my faults
With ready admittance and acceptance.
Replace my anger at myself
With understanding and humility;
My guilt at what I've done
With your loving forgiveness;
My despair about improving
With hope in your power.
And above all, Lord, may I accept the
    weaknesses in myself;
May I bring them to you and ask your help
In growing through them to become a
    stronger person,
Strong in forgiveness,
Strong in acceptance of forgiveness
From you and others.

22 FALLING IN LOVE

I've fallen in love, Lord:
Someone I used to notice a lot.
I suppose I fancied her,
And now I know she fancies me, too.
It's a good feeling — I like it.
It's like the sun shining again after cloudy
    weather,
Or a light going on in a dim room.
The attraction is growing after these two weeks.

I like her, Lord.
I thank you for your gifts to her,
Her easy personality and good looks.
It's easy to talk with her;
Thanks for our conversations.

Thanks, Lord, for the relationship as it is now.
Don't let me ruin it with my selfishness,
Or let the sexual attraction become over-important.

I know I need her, Lord.
Sometimes I'm afraid that my needs are
    stronger than the depth of my love.
I fear being alone, and I don't want that to be
    the reason for continuing to meet her.

I want to love and be loved:
It's like the attraction of the wave to the shore.
Sometimes I'm more intent on receiving than
    giving.
I don't want to hurt her, but I'm selfish.

Be with me, Lord, and be with us in our
    friendship.
Be present in our times together,
Building our love,
Nourishing what's good in us,
Giving us a glimpse of what love is like,
A hint of what you are like.

23 SEXUAL ATTRACTION

Lord, my feelings for my girlfriend are really
    strong,
And hers for me.
Our physical attraction is intense,
And at times this puts a strain on our
    relationship.
We feel drawn towards a bodily expression
    that we know deep-down
Is not right for us,
That is appropriate only in a relationship more
    committed than ours.

I thank you, Lord, for this friendship and love.
I ask your help for us in controlling our sexual
    attraction.
I want to show affection and love —
(Although often I'm afraid of it) —
And I also want to show my respect
For her and for myself.

Help us, Lord, to be honest with each other,
To admit our real feelings and desires for each
    other;
And help us not to confuse the intensity of
    our sexual feelings
With either the depth of our love
Or the level of our commitment.
We are experiencing many feelings together:
        our feelings of love and our sexual
            attraction,
        our feelings of fear or of anger,

our feelings of hope and doubt.
Let all these feelings brighten, and not shadow,
   our love.

You have given each of us, Lord, the power to love,
The grace to sympathise with each other,
And you have made us man and woman so that
   we are powerfully attracted to each other.
Help true friendship and real love to grow in
   our relationship.
Lord, be present with us in our love.

24 STANDING OUT IN A GROUP

Lord, at times it's difficult to stand out in the
   crowd,
It's difficult to speak out in a group.
I want to be honest,
But to stand out tears at my deep desire to be
   accepted,
Brings out my fears of being alone,
Of having no friends.
I love many of my friends;
It's just that I don't always agree with what
   they do and say.
I'm like a tree growing one way, and they want
   me to grow in another.

Sometimes I follow their way;
I treat people badly in what I say or do,
Cheat someone of his good name,

Say the unkind thing to the girl everyone is
    unkind to,
Drink too much,
Or try drugs,
Just to be one of them.

Lord, I know you understand this.
You can even see into the depths of my heart,
And know why I do what I do.
Help me to remain in the group, but not
    controlled by it.

You know, Lord, that I need friends,
And my needs are sometimes stronger than my
    beliefs.
Help me to be open to what others want,
Understanding of weakness,
And courageous also to do what I know is right.

25 MORNING PRAYER

Thank you, Lord, for this day;
For the dawn which is a sign of the
sureness of your love,
        your presence,
        your forgiveness,
        your companionship,
All the days of our lives.

I start this day in trust in you, Lord.
It may be ordinary,
A day of work or study or even drudgery;
I give it to you.

I offer you the hours of this day,
That now or later they may be in your service.

I pray for those I will meet.
May I bring in some small way
A dawning of joy and peace in their lives.

Thank you, Lord, for this day;
May I always be thankful for what is good.

26 EVENING PRAYER

This evening, Lord, I give you thanks.

For the good things of today,
 for people whose friendship I value,
 for the work well done,
 for deadlines met,
 for home and for shelter,
 for the food I ate,
Thank you, Lord.

May the darkness of tonight
Take with it the bitterness of today;
May sunset put to rest my anger,
And the starlight be a reminder that your
 forgiveness never fails.
For my failure in your service this day,
I ask your forgiveness, Lord.

I see now that you were present to me this day;
In the love of those I met,
In the call to sympathise and console,

[41]

In the cries of those poorer than I —
Those who have no friends,
No food, no home, no shelter.
I remember them now, Lord, in your presence.

For today, Lord, thanks and sorry.
I put to rest with you the troubles of this day;
I ask the peace of your presence until the new
    day dawns.
May the protection you give at the end of a day
Be with me and my loved ones
All the days of our lives.

27 CHRISTMAS PRAYER

I pray, Lord, that the simplicity of your presence
Will bring to birth in me and in others
        a compassion for the poor,
        a hunger for justice among the oppressed,
        and a real desire for brotherhood among
            nations.

May this Christmas be a time of
        sincere reconciliation,
        lasting forgiveness,
        deep-rooted joy.

May it be the smile of God,
And the fragrance of your holy presence among
    us all.

Thank you, Lord, for coming among us.

POSTSCRIPT

The joys and sorrows, struggles and hopes of our lives are the material of prayer. The exhilaration of friendship and of success, the disappointment of let-down and failure: all of these and many other experiences can be opportunities for perceiving God's presence and call in our lives.

The years of youth are a time of variety of experience. Many questions are new and they all seem to come together — questions about yourself, your world, and God. You meet people and begin to respond to them in more complex ways. Your relationship with parents changes. You find yourself moved strongly with differing hopes and desires. All is matter for prayer. All is part of your relationship with God. Relationships grow as secrets are shared, and the secrets of our lives can be occasions for God to share the secrets of his relationship with us.

You have probably identified with some of the experiences on which these prayers are based. Not all of them, however, will have struck you as equally authentic for yourself. At times you may feel you cannot honestly say such words — for example, if you have been badly hurt and cannot yet say words of forgiveness with God. In that case, don't pray what is untrue for you. Pray over your hurt, or pray for the help of God to forgive.

Some of these prayers can be said today; some may be more appropriate later on. Like many religious words and songs, we learn them not just for the time being, but for a time in the future when we might need them.

From the prayers about morning, evening and Christmas, you can see that special times of the day or year, or special occasions, can be opportunities for welcoming God's presence into our lives. These can be happy or sad times, good memories or painful recollections. For the person of faith, they are instances of prayer and of a deep awareness of God's friendship.

Some moments are almost universally acknowledged as "carriers of God's presence". Sunrise, noon and sunset are sacred times in many cultures. Catholics have always marked these hours by the Angelus bell. Hindus take a ritual bath, or pray while bowing to the four corners of the universe, recognising the presence of God in the north, south, east and west.

We are reminded that God is at work in our lives by human events such as birth, illness, and, of course, the sad and lonely moment of death. Birthdays, too, can be seen as times of "visitation" from God. Any incident that deeply involves our feelings, hopes, memories, fears or anxieties can be an opportunity for meeting God.

Try to adapt these prayers to suit your own experiences, or compose some for yourself. They will help you to get in touch with the moments and experiences in which you will find God.

3
PRAYING WITH HOPES
AND DESIRES

28 FUTURE PRAYER

I often wonder, Lord, what my life will be like.

Right now it seems simple enough:
I'm at school, I'm studying.
Exams will come soon; I pray for success.
I think of different jobs or careers —
Nursing, teaching, medicine, secretary,
    technician;
Will I change my mind?
Will I have enough points?
I'm like a wisp of smoke wafting through the air;
Life is fairly straightforward now, but where
        will the future bring me?

There's a new world before me;
I will meet new people, make new friends.
If I suffer hurts, feel down,
How well will I cope?
How will I react to success and wealth,
Or poverty?

Will I become hard and mean,
Or will I share?
Whom will I marry?
Will we have children?
How will we get on?

At times, Lord, it all seems so exciting;
Other times, I'm scared stiff.

I wonder about things I have no control over —
War and lasting peace, our economic situation,
Unemployment and prosperity, death and life.
Will I hold on to you, the God of my youth,
Or will my faith in you be weakened and lost?

Lord, help me to trust your presence in the
    mystery of life.
I know I can trust you.
I know I can rely on you to be there, always.
In all this uncertainty, only you, Christ
    God, are sure.
You're like a rock, facing wave and surf, and
    never overcome.
You're a friend, solid and loyal.
Be near me, Lord,
Guide me.
Nurture in me, Lord, this gift of trust.

29 AN INDIAN PRAYER

Lord, may your love play upon my voice,
and rest in my silence.
Let it pass through my heart,
into all that I do.
Let your love shine like stars in the darkness of
   my sleep,
and in the dawn at my awakening.
Let it burn in all the flames of my desires,
and flow in all the currents of my love.
Let me carry your love in my life,
as a harp does its music,
and give it back to you at last with my life.

(Based on a poem by Tagore)

30 CONFLICTING DESIRES

I have so many conflicting desires, Lord,
Or that's how it seems.
One moment I'm all for good,
Then I turn nasty and selfish.
At other times I really want to help another,
A friend or a parent,
And I'm loving and tolerant.

Then again I'm filled with prejudice and I want
   to throw my weight around.
Why have I conflicting desires?

Lord, nourish within me the good desires,
The desires for a wholesome love,
Concern for the needy,
Desire for prayer with you;
And in the silence of my personality, Lord,
Make strong my good desires.

31 DESIRE TO LOVE

My desire to love someone is very strong, Lord;
Without a close friend, I feel incomplete.
I want to give the love that's in my heart to
    someone,
And I want to be loved in return.
It's like a river flowing in circles looking for
    the sea,
Or roots growing underneath the ground
    stretching out for water;
I strain at loving and being loved.
My heart wants to give itself,
And hear another heart echoing its love.

Thanks for the desire; it's from you.
You are the source of all love, and of our
    desire for love.

Help me, Lord, to be in control of these
    feelings.

This desire can lead me into blind alleys.
Sometimes I give myself just to have a friend;
(I sometimes think it's better to have any kind
    of relationship than none at all).

Sometimes I give in to physical desires which
    are devoid of love.
Help me, Lord, so that this desire to love will
    lead to love,
Not exploitation and frustration.

Give me patience, Lord.
If I search I will find real love,
And I will give real love.
The desire to love will surely lead me very close
    to you
In kindness and in compassion,
Or very far from you, in selfish, greedy love.
Help me, guide me, show me how to love.
Show me how to love with your love.

32 HONEST RELATIONSHIPS

We seem to be at our best, Lord,
What we meet in an atmosphere
In which each one's talents can emerge,
Rather than trying to pretend we're happier or
    more talented than we are.
I like it best when I'm in an honest group,
Where we treat each other as persons, not
    possessions;
Where we give people the benefit of a question,
Rather than a judgement of condemnation;
Where the way we get along together brings
    freedom;

[49]

Where each person is allowed the time to grow
    into his own personality;
Where no masks are worn or pretences played
    out.

I thank you, Lord, for the people I find this
    freedom with.
Our desires are deeper than we often admit;
We want to find people who will accept us,
Not for our parents' name or address,
But as we are.
Our desires are for a life deeper than the
    boisterousness of drink
Or the unreality of drugs.

When I find a group that's honest and genuine,
It's like finding fresh air in the smog of a city,
Or a cool breeze on a humid day.
It's great, and I feel free and thankful.
I feel hopeful.

Lord, help me to be the type of person to
    support such a group,
Even if it's painful.

You have given me this desire;
Nourish it within me,
Make strong its roots,
Make plentiful its fruits.

33 DESIRE TO HELP IN THE WORLD

Lord,
The film I just saw was about the miseries and
    injustices of the world;
The headlines in the newspapers report violence,
    murder, death;
And I think of other particular suffering
    around us:
        thousands of children sick in India,
        death and loneliness in Belfast,
        drug-addicts exploited by pushers,
        kids hooked on glue,
        ignorance through lack of education,
        sickness through lack of medical care,
        death on the streets.

Lord, how can I respond to the cries of your
    people?

I think of the less-known sufferings:
The anxieties and depressions of lonely men
    and women;
Of those who attempt suicide;
Of those who drown their cares in over-
    indulgence in alcohol.

What can I do to help?
I want to, Lord,
I want my life to be a channel of your love to
        them;
But what can one man, one woman, do?

Help me, Lord, to believe that I can help,
And give me the courage and generosity to
     offer myself in service,
That my life might be like a candle,
Giving light to others.

34 FOR COMPASSION

I pray for the gift of compassion, Lord.
I ask for the ability to enter into the feelings of
     another
With love,
And for the generosity to make no judgement on
     another's life,
Even if this tries my patience.
And in all this I experience the joy of knowing
     that in compassion
I am like you,
The God of compassion.

35 TO DO WHAT IS GOOD WITH
MY LIFE

Lord, I really want to do something good with
     my life.
I see the needs of the world I'm part of,
     one million poor in my own country,
     people killed each day through violence,
     old people living lonely and in squalour,
     kids of my own age drugging themselves as
     an escape from life.

I know there are needs,
There are people who cannot live
Without the dedicated help of your friends.

I hear your call,
Sometimes a whisper, other times a gentle shout,
Inviting me to be your presence,
Through my own personality and my own talents,
And with all my weaknesses,
In the world of these people.
But, Lord, I'm afraid.
    I don't know if I can do anything for them.
    I don't know how you want me to follow you:
    Married? single? a religious? a priest?
I'm not sure I can give without losing so much
    myself.

Faith is what I ask, and light and love:
Faith to believe in your risen power at the foot
    of your cross,
Light to know the way you're asking me to
    serve you,
And love to trust that it's all possible.

36 MAKING A PRAYER WITH DESIRE

Sit or lie in a position in which you are comfort-
able, in a place, indoors or outdoors, where you
can be silent and quiet. Give yourself a few
moments to become inwardly still by breathing

deeply and rhythmically. Then, when you are
ready, imagine yourself lying on a raft in the
middle of a river . . . a sunny day. . . . Notice the
wind on your face . . . on your hands . . . the heat
of the sun on your body . . . the sounds you hear
of flowing water, wind, birds . . . smells of the
river . . . blossoms. . . . Watch the river flowing
past you . . . slow in one place, fast in another. . . .
Change your focus now and allow your various
desires to flow through you. . . . Notice them, no
judgements . . . desires to be liked . . . desires to
be successful . . . any others . . . desires for power
. . . wealth . . . prestige . . . revenge. . . . Name one
of your good desires. . . . Tell this desire to
Christ. . . . See that desire flowing near you,
written on a piece of wood floating on the
river. . . . Pick up the piece of wood. . . . How do
you feel when you're looking at it?. . . Share your
feelings with Christ. . . . What has he to say to
you? . . . Let the piece of wood flow with the
river and allow your imagination to flow into the
future and to where this desire might lead
you. . . . Speak to Christ about it. . . . Let him be
with you as it unfolds in the future. . . . Give to
him the fears and anxieties you feel. . . . Thank
the Lord for your "holy" desire. . . . Again
imagine yourself on the raft. . . . Listen again to
the sounds around you. . . . Become aware of your
position, sitting, squatting, or lying down. . . .
Thank the Lord for this prayer. . . . Stand up and
end your prayer.

POSTSCRIPT

The section you have just prayed through introduces you to the world of your desires. Each of us possesses a mixture of varying desires, wishes and hopes. Some of our desires are acceptable to us; others we prefer to hide. We have desires to help others, to be loving and to be compassionate, to do good and avoid evil. But we have other desires too, like revenge and aggression, which we often try to hide. All of these desires can be brought to God, as the previous section shows.

Many religious peoples, not just Christians, practise this "prayer of holy desires". We might call them holy hopes or wishes, as the word "desire" in our culture can have connotations of desire for revenge, for exploitation of others, or other negative meanings.

We can pray with our holy desires, knowing that they are planted within us by God and grow with his help. Our relationship with him can in fact nourish, intensify, increase and multiply these wishes, so that our heart is filled with them rather than with negative desires. In praying over them we grow them, like sunshine and water nourish a plant.

Bringing our good desires to God in prayer also helps us to overcome our resistance to acting them out, as many of them go against the selfishness that is within us.

You may be able to identify with some of the hopes expressed in the preceding prayers. Allow them to reach your own good desires, and in your

own words bring them to God. Trust your good
desires, for they will bring you, and others, to a
fuller friendship with God.

4
PRAYING FOR OTHERS

37   FOR ONE IN TROUBLE

Lord, I pray for him,
His alcoholism is a serious affliction for himself
    and a heartbreak to those near to him.
Let him know that you love him and forgive his
    weaknesses.
Give him the knowledge to accept the help that
    others would like to give.

His illness is causing him guilt and anxiety;
Let him know we care for him.

May we who love him, or who are involved in
    his life,
Know how to help him in a constructive way.
May we be supportive and caring towards him,
Showing him through our sympathy and concern
Some of your love and care for him.

38 FOR A FRIEND

Lord, I want to pray for her,
She's going through a rough time.
Help her with some peace of mind;
Give her the direction to find a new path
    through her dilemma.
I thank you for her,
I thank you for our friendship.
I want to be a real support to her in her life,
And with this problem.
Help me to listen to her,
And to be straight in my own responses.
Bless our friendship;
May we build up each other's talents and
    goodness,
And may our friendship with each other
Be a sign that we share in your love.

39 A FRIEND'S BIRTHDAY

Lord, today I pray for my friend on his birthday;
Give him your best blessings on this day;
May he know that you love him.

Let our greetings bring him joy,
And our good wishes assure him of our
    friendship.
Be with him in his new year and all his life,
        companion in joy,
        peace in anxieties,
        courage in fear;
Give him confidence and hope.

Develop in him the qualities that are good,
Forgive his weaknesses,
Pardon his selfishness.
Let him look on himself as you look on him,
You who made him;
Your very own creation,
More precious than an angel.

Your blessings be upon him.

40   FOR ONE WHO IS ILL

Lord, she whom you love is ill.

You well know her pain, her suffering and her fear.
Give her again the joy of good health,
But, more so, give her now the assurance that
    you are close;
Let her know the presence of your love.
Give peace of heart and confidence to all of us
    who care for her;
May we glimpse in her suffering and pain
The gifts of courage you have given her.
Help us to be hopeful that her serious illness
    will pass.
Strengthen her body, mind and spirit,
To be fully with us again.

41   WHEN A LOVED ONE IS DYING

Lord, be with us in these days of illness.

In our anxiety and fear,
Let us know that death is the dawning of
    eternal life.
Give our brother freedom from pain,
And give him peace in his anxiety.
Hold your cross before his eyes,
For this is the sign of resurrection and life.

We fear illness and death;
We are anxious for him and for ourselves.
Lord Jesus, may we experience
In these dark moments
The closeness of your friendship.
May we know and feel the presence of your
    Father,
Strengthening us.

POSTSCRIPT

Prayer for others is a way of entering into a relationship with God. We believe that God is intimately
concerned with the life of each person; to pray for
someone is to join with God in his care for another's
life.

Prayer is also a way of becoming more tolerant of
other people and of opening ourselves to knowing
and understanding others. It is a way of loving. It is

also a trusting in God: we make known our prayer for another and leave the answering to God. He may, in fact, answer our prayers in a way we do not expect.

When a prayer isn't answered, as when we pray for a parent to stop drinking and she doesn't, or when we pray to pass an exam and we fail, or we pray for someone to fall in love with us and he doesn't, we might react in many ways. We might give up on God. Or we might realise that much of what we ask is in the power of people to give us, like peace in a country depends on the people's efforts to live in peace. Or we can respond by allowing our trust in God to grow so that despite what we now feel, we know that he is not letting us down.

The prayers in this section are examples of how you might pray for someone. Include names of people close to you. Include different reasons for praying for someone; for example, the prayer on alcoholism could be for any number of other intentions you would pray for: drug-addiction, infidelity, gambling. These prayers will help you compose your own. They will also invite you to share the love of God in your relationship with the people you pray for. We often wonder how we might soften or improve our attitudes to another person: try praying for them and see if there is any difference.

5
PRAYING WITH SCRIPTURE

The gospel stories are meeting-points for prayer between God and man. People of all ages find in them mirrors of their own relationship with God, and reflections in Christ of how God deals with us. The following chapter gives a method of using gospel stories for personal prayer, and indicates stories from the gospel which might be used for prayer. By reading the gospels slowly you can find your own favourite passages and build up a reservoir of stories from the life of Christ to which you can return in the prayer-moments of your life.

Each story should become like a favourite place for you. People have places — maybe at the sea or in the mountains, or in a park in a city — to which they go if they want refreshment and relaxation. These are places in which they can leave aside the trivialities of life and return to their centre. Gospel stories can also be like this; they are powerful memories of the life of Christ to which his followers return to centre their prayer-life, in times of joy and of sorrow. The mere memory of them brings the presence of God to mind, like the memory of a honeymoon place can bring alive once again for a married couple the reality of their love.

Try this way of praying the gospel. Use the stories here; discover your own. Nourish your prayer-life with the great stories of the Christian people; through them allow Christ to speak personally to you. Share these stories and your reactions to them with others, so that the pages of the gospel become carriers for you of the grace of the living God and risen Christ.

JOHN 6: 16-21

The Calm and the Storm

Read the story and then try to imagine it in its various details. See the different people in the boat; a stormy sea and a boat tossing around; wind and rain; people bailing water. Hear the shouts of fear; some argument about what to do. They notice Jesus over on the shore, a figure in the fog; he walks over to the boat; hear his words. Their fear lifts and they make their way to the other shore.

That evening the disciples went down to the shore of the lake and got into a boat to make for Capernaum on the other side of the lake. It was getting dark by now and Jesus had still not rejoined them. The wind was strong, and the sea was getting rough. They had rowed three or four miles when they saw Jesus walking on the lake and coming towards the boat. This frightened them, but he said, "It is I. Do not be afraid". They were for taking him into the boat, but in no time it reached the shore at the place they were making for.

Now imagine yourself in the boat. Your feelings about the storm: fear or some confidence?

You look over the boat and see Jesus, you hear his words; how do you feel?

Think now of storms in your own life: your fears or resentments, your anxieties.

Tell Jesus your feelings, hear his words.

Talk with him or stay in silence with him.

Tell him how you feel with him and ask him for what you want.

Let him move off; how do you feel now?

Talk with him again if you want: ask him for a gift he can give, like peace of mind, confidence in yourself, forgiveness of someone who hurts you.

End your prayer with a prayer of praise.

This is a well-tried and popular way of praying the gospel. It puts you in touch both with Jesus and with people who might be like yourself. Use your imagination to put yourself in the place and in the mood of someone in the story, and then talk to Jesus from that point of view. The memory of the gospel incident brings you to prayer from your own present mood and state of mind. It is not a returning to the past, it is a method of allowing the Jesus of the gospel pages to become the Jesus of your life's pages. You might look up some of the following passages and use them when you feel like one or more of the people in the story.

Ashamed With Christ

This is the story of a woman caught committing adultery and brought to Jesus by some people who were trying to catch him out on a point of religious law. Use the story to pray when you feel ashamed or guilty over some sin or sins, identifying with the woman, or when you feel you are blaming someone, or judging another very harshly, identifying with one of the accusers. In each situation hear the words of Jesus addressed to you: "I do not condemn you; go away and sin no more".

The scribes and the Pharisees brought a woman along who had been caught committing adultery; and making her stand there in full view of everybody, they said to Jesus, "Master, this woman was caught in the very act of committing adultery, and Moses has ordered us in the Law to condemn women like this to death by stoning. What have you to say?" They asked him this as a test, looking for something to use against him. But Jesus bent down and started writing on the ground with his finger. As they persisted with their question, he looked up and said, "If there is one of you who has not sinned, let him be the first to throw a stone at her". Then he bent down and wrote on the ground again. When they heard this they went away one by one, beginning with the eldest, until Jesus was left alone with the woman, who remained standing there. He looked up and said, "Woman, where are they? Has no one condemned you?" "No one, Sir", she replied. "Neither do I condemn you," said Jesus, "go away and don't sin any more."

MARK 4: 35-41

Another Storm and Another Calm

This is a story similar to John 6: 16-21. Pray it in a similar way. Its difference is that Jesus is asleep in the boat, so you might pray over it at a time when Jesus seems "asleep", non-helpful, in your life.

With the coming of evening that same day, he said to them, "Let us cross over to the other side". And leaving the crowd behind they took him, just as he was, in the boat; and there were other boats with him. Then it began to blow a gale and the waves were breaking into the boat so that it was almost swamped. But he was in the stern, his head on the cushion, asleep. They woke him and said to him, "Master, do you not care? We are going down!" And he woke up and rebuked the wind and said to the sea, "Quiet now! Be calm!" And the wind dropped, and all was calm again. Then he said to them, "Why are you so frightened? How is it that you have no faith?" They were filled with awe and said to one another, "Who can this be? Even the wind and the sea obey him".

Hurt in Friendship

A story you might pray when you feel very let down by a friend. In it you might identify with Jesus who was let down by Peter. Talk over with him what it's like to be let down. Allow him to console you with the knowledge that he does not let you down and that he knows what you're going through. Pray for the gift to forgive as he could forgive Peter. Forgiveness will not necessarily come immediately, but your prayer is a beginning of forgiveness, and of freedom for yourself.

They seized him then and led him away, and they took him to the high priest's house. Peter followed at a distance. They had lit a fire in the middle of the courtyard and Peter sat down among them, and as he was sitting there by the blaze a servant-girl saw him, peered at him, and said, "This person was with him too". But he denied it. "Woman," he said, "I do not know him". Shortly afterwards someone else saw him and said, "You are another of them". But Peter replied, "I am not, my friend". About an hour later another man insisted saying, "This fellow was certainly with him. Why, he is a Galilean". "My friend," said Peter, "I do not know what you are talking about". At that instant, while he was still speaking, the cock crew, and the Lord turned and looked straight at Peter, and Peter remembered what the Lord had said to him, "Before the cock crows today, you will have disowned me three times". And he went outside and wept bitterly.

JOHN 2: 1-10   Wedding Joy

A story for a time when you feel very joyful. Identify with the bride or the groom, and with their happiness in their love. And with the fact that Jesus shares their joy. Allow him to increase your joy by sharing it with him. (Your joy need not be the joy of a relationship; you can pray with this scene any happy experience in your life — of friendship, success, creativity - allowing Jesus to be part of your happiness.)

Three days later there was a wedding at Cana in Galilee. The mother of Jesus was there, and Jesus and his disciples had also been invited. When they ran out of wine, since the wine provided for the wedding was all finished, the mother of Jesus said to him, "They have no wine". Jesus said, "Woman, why turn to me? My hour has not yet come". His mother said to the servants, "Do whatever he tells you". There were six stone water jars standing there, meant for the ablutions that are customary among the Jews: each could hold twenty or thirty gallons. Jesus said to the servants, "Fill the jars with water", and they filled them to the brim. "Draw some out now", he told them, "and take it to the steward". They did this; the steward tasted the water, and it had turned into wine. Having no idea where it came from — only the servants who had drawn the water knew — the steward called the bridegroom and said, "People generally serve the best wine first, and keep the cheaper sort till the guests have had plenty to drink; but you have kept the best wine till now".

[69]

6
PRAYING WITH PRAISE
AND THANKS

42 A PRAYER OF PRAISE

For mountains, sea and sky —
a glimpse of your beauty and eternity,
I praise you, Lord,
For their grandeur and power.

For men and women, friends and companions —
a glimpse of your goodness and care,
I praise and thank you, Lord.

For Jesus, in life and death,
I praise and thank you, Lord;
For the security of your presence,
    your life,
    your love.

For those whose only mountains are garbage-
    heaps to search for food;
For those whose only sea is the open sewer in a
    slum;

For those who never see the sky except through
    polluted air;
For those to whom animals are not pets,
But either a nuisance to be fed or the guarded
    source of children's milk;
For those whose only birdsong is a cry of
    despair or wail of poverty,
And for whom the flesh of a fishbone would
    be a luxury in a week's begging;
For those whose only comfort in life is
    friendship —
At least they haven't lost what is most essential;
And for those whose only companionship is the
    cut-throat competitiveness of the city's wealth;
Lord, I pray.

May I find you, Lord, within your poor,
May I hear your call and your cry,
May I work with you for your brothers and
    sisters;
Only then does my praise for mountains,
        for sea and sky,
        for men and women,
        and for Jesus,
Ring true.

43 NEW BIRTH

Thanks, Lord, for my new brother;
The cries are a welcome sound in our house,
And all the inconvenience of the past months
    is now a joy.
We waited those months, and now say thanks
    for his safe arrival.

Lord, I often just look at him and marvel at the
    gift of human life;
His body seems knit together with such care
    and intelligence.
His helplessness brings my prayer to you for him.

I thank you for the mystery of human life,
For this child born of my parents' love and into
    our family.
I ask of you all good things for him:
        good health so he'll grow strong,
        a life that's joyful and full of meaning,
        friends who will develop his talents and
            goodness.

Just now, Lord, I ask everything good for him.
I hope he'll always find love and be thankful;
I hope that he'll have enough of the world's goods,
But not so much that he'll get selfish.
I hope that in all of life's moments he'll know
        you as a companion,
        joy in the good times,
        comfort and help in times of trouble.

44 THANKS FOR A SKILL

Thanks, Lord, for the skill of playing music.
I feel pleased with myself;
The hours of practice have been worthwhile.
It's wonderful to be able to express myself like
 this.
In a way I'm being creative,
I'm sharing your power of creation;
 a new song,
 a new picture,
 a new love,
Are all part of your continual creation in the
 world.

I want to use my skill in your service, Lord.
Help me to enrich the lives of others with it.
What you have given me, I return to you,
Lovingly shaped and formed by my own hands.

Thank you, Lord.
Play your loving and creating through me.

45 A JOB

I've got a job, Lord;
Not just for the summer, but a permanent job.
Thanks.

Those days of fruitless searching were
    becoming frustrating.
I need the employment, and I'm glad I can help
    out at home.
It's like finding the way out of a dead-end or a
    cul-de-sac;
Everything seems brighter now, Lord.

Help me share some of this joy,
Especially with those whose lives are less happy.

46 THANKS FOR FRIENDS

I thank you, Lord, for a good friend:
His patience and willingness to listen are a good
    example to me.
In the rush and bustle of my life,
In my anxieties over exams and jobs,
He reminds me that people are more important
    than projects;

For another friend whose company I enjoy,
And whose friendship brings laughter to my joy
And sympathy in sorrow;
She teaches me that it's good to be friends;

For one whom I admire:
His commitment to his work and study, even
    in times without enthusiasm,
Teaches me that it's worth striving for excellence;

And for yet another:
As we share our hopes and dreams for the
    future,
We nourish our desires to live our lives in the
    spirit of the Gospel,
And strengthen the Christian roots of our
    society;

For a friend
Who seems to pray much and remind me that
    God is near;

And for another
Who is ill with cancer,
And whose bravery, patience and good humour
Teach me how to die —
And I know I'll need that lesson some day.

Thank you, Lord, for all these and many more.

POSTSCRIPT

These are prayers of thanks to God for the gifts we
appreciate. It is a way of praying that we can always
use. Even in moments of personal trouble we can
thank God for the good things in the world. It is a
means of lifting our eyes and spirits outside
ourselves. It is being able to thank the Lord for the

sun shining behind a grey cloud, or for the peaceful water beneath the waves that are ruffled on the surface. The day you thank God for the colour and smell of a rose can be when you glimpse that God is ever active in our world; and then, because of praise for a rose, your faith will never grow weary!

There is also praise from within ourselves, in the moments of friendship and of joy when life is good, or when love is flowing well between ourselves and another. A prayer of thanks and praise for what is good in our lives can in fact deepen our thankfulness.

Pray these examples of praise-prayers. Pause within them and add your own words. Make your own prayers of praise and thanks for what you want deep-down to thank God most for.

But what about the times you don't feel like praising? Our prayers have shown that you can bring all your experiences to God. The prayers of praise evoke a faith that within all personal darkness is the light of God. It's like believing in the glimmer of the lighthouse on a foggy night, or trusting in the radar scan in the dark. It means that your faith in God depends not only on your feelings; the prayer of praise lets God be God. It is a prayer that looks at his world and at your own life and says that no matter what the world looks like, God is beautiful, powerful, loving. Finally it is a prayer of deep faith that while roses can bloom anywhere, only the eyes of faith can see them in their full beauty.